Take
The
Initiative

Carol A. Nero

Copyright © by Carol A. Nero 2022. All rights reserved.

Before this document is duplicated or reproduced in any manner, the publisher's consent must be gained. Therefore, the contents within can neither be stored electronically, transferred, nor kept in a database. Neither in Part nor full can the document be copied, scanned, faxed, or retained without approval from the publisher or creator.

Table of Contents

Unsteady and unprepared

Reading, analyzing, and having conversations about good leadership are much simpler activities than actually performing such roles. The realm of leadership is one in which there are no correct answers, difficult dialogues, the establishment of an unknown course, the influence of others, and the possibility of unpredictable events. Taking responsibility for the future of your company and the people who work there carries with it a weight that may either derail our plans or be channeled into productive endeavors, depending on how it is managed. Nevertheless, there is no such thing as a successful endeavor that does not involve blunders, setbacks, obstacles, and defeats along the road. Being a leader needs having bravery, and having courage takes a certain type of being vulnerable. Courageous leadership requires four distinct skill sets.

Vulnerable and Roiling with Uncertainty

You can't get to courage without rumbling with vulnerability. This is having the guts to show up fully even when you can't control how things will turn out. Being vulnerable in your connections with other people requires you to do so in every meeting, email, phone call, and face-to-face contact that you have, both inside and outside of the office. Being vulnerable has been described as having feelings of both excitement and fear at the same moment. You have this overwhelming sense that you have to act or speak, but a part of you is telling you that it might not be wise to do either of those things right now. It requires courage to hold off on taking action and instead jump into a coaching dialogue with a team member so you can help them find the solutions themselves. This frame of thinking is required in order for leaders to successfully engage in challenging conversations and provide feedback that is both honest and useful on a consistent basis. When it comes to offering comments or suggestions, keep the following in mind:

• When you put an emphasis on clarity, you boost trust while also reducing unproductive behavior. Being transparent fosters greater connection as well as empathy. Clarity also establishes a boundary, which enables the other person to choose how to proceed with the feedback after it has been provided.

• It's important to be aware of your own triggers. Do you make an effort to take control of the situation, protect yourself, or start people-pleasing when you've been triggered? Having this knowledge can assist you in moving into a position of choice so that you can step into vulnerability.

Living Your Values (Rather Than Simply Professing Them)

First, you should be clear on what your views are, and then you should make sure that your actions, thoughts, and words are consistent with those values. Create a written record of your values and give them a name. The next step is to determine the fundamental actions that are representative of how you might live those ideals. And what kinds of actions should you be looking out for that indicate you're getting off track?

Never be afraid to speak your mind when confronted with a challenging situation if you are a courageous leader who actually lives their values rather than just talking about them. As an illustration, bold leaders do not engage in the practice of willful blindness. If you want to be a good leader, you need to be aware of what's going on in the world around you. You need to have the awareness to know when to act and the knowledge that you may occasionally be required to act in challenging circumstances. Recognizing these possibilities for leadership and setting an example for your team both need a certain amount of bravery on your part. Because acting morally is rarely simple, coming to conclusions that are consistent with your values will be challenging for you.

Braving Trust (And Being The First To Trust)

Now, let me make it clear that I am not arguing for blind trust, which is defined as a mix of a strong propensity to trust and/or the absence of limiting consideration. I'm referring to the practice of intelligent trust, which combines sound business judgment with sound judgment about other people in order to improve one's gut instinct and intuition. The state of being vulnerable does not come before trust. In point of fact, they are inseparable companions. In order to cultivate trust in a relationship, it is necessary to expose oneself to discomfort on a regular basis and also to make the conscious decision to prioritize bravery over ease. To be a leader who is trusted and trusted by others, you must be someone who others can rely on to do what you say you will do, which includes operating within the scope of your abilities and the constraints you face. Take responsibility for your actions and make amends. When there is a mistake made, accountability means that you are willing to question yourself, "What part did I play in this?" when there is a mistake made.

Last but not least, just because someone is vulnerable does not mean that they have to entirely open up and let down their guard. On the other hand, establishing clear limits for both yourself and your team can help create a climate that is conducive to trust.

How To Get To The Top

When things aren't going well for you, the way you talk to yourself about it affects a great deal. Finding fault demonstrates a fixed attitude, while trying to improve one's performance for the next experience demonstrates a growth mindset. When something goes wrong, it is important to analyze the situation and determine what facts are present as well as what interpretations are being used to fill in the blanks. Recognize the feeling that comes up for you, and then investigate it with a curious mind. Be aware of every time one of the three most harmful tales enters your mind: those that undermine your merit, your faith, or your ability to create.

The ability to choose how one reacts when confronted with fear is the single most crucial component of brave leadership. Are you going to put everything on autopilot and try to protect, control, or appease the people?

Remember to rumble with vulnerability the next time you are asked to lead bravely. This means showing up fully, embodying your beliefs, being the first to trust, and learning to rise when things don't go according to plan.

Remorse and sympathy

Trust is an essential component of successful teamwork. We rely on the production crew, our musicians, our pastor, and many others in the chain in order to carry out our duties in the worship ministry. When anything breaks down in the middle of service, it may have a catastrophic effect on the people on your team. Being the one to break the chain is never a pleasant experience for anyone involved. It is much more troubling when members of your team start to question the validity of their beliefs or their position within the church. During the pandemic, worship services are the most apparent way in which the church is losing its face. As a result, many worship pastors find themselves in a difficult position today. The strain that comes from having church members with varying points of view is something that pastors have to deal with. Either they are upset with their pastor because the pastor canceled worship services or they are frustrated with themselves because they are not doing enough.

This is the environment that a team leader must navigate in 2021. When there are the hardships of everyday life to be attended to, in addition to a pandemic and societal instability, the recipe is ripe for shame to appear on the scene. Shame is the sensation that we are in the wrong, not the problems themselves. It is entirely our fault. There is a feeling of shame. Either we are ashamed of ourselves, or we are projecting that feeling onto other people. Even worse is the fact that we live our lives unconscious of it.

The feeling of shame is destructive to teamwork and can even lead to abusive behavior.

It is possible to induce the uncomfortable feeling of humiliation in every member of the team. For instance, when things are not going as planned, leaders frequently resort to shaming their followers in order to put everyone in their place. Shaming a member of the team for being late to a rehearsal makes the situation more on the individual's lack of responsibility rather than an issue that needs to be resolved. As leaders, we face the temptation to insult and use humiliation as a bargaining chip in order to get what we want.

Our path. However, shame is a barrier to healthy teamwork and a threat to the existence of community. Put an end to the feeling of shame. To begin, an assault on a person's feeling of worth can be understood as an example of shame. The more we shame and condemn one another, the deeper our wounds get. Because of this, ultimately, shame is the enemy of working together as a team.

The best way to combat the damaging effects of shame is with the ally of empathy.

The antidote to shame is empathy. The important thing is to try to think of things that are not related to oneself. To give one example, feelings of shame and guilt are not the same thing. When we feel guilty, we turn our eyes outside and seek techniques to undo the harm that we have done." When we are embarrassed, our attention is drawn inward, and we concentrate primarily on the feelings that are boiling within us rather than paying attention to what is occurring in the world around us. It is one thing to feel awful about things we can change, like the problem of arriving late to events, for example. To inflict shame, with the intention of creating scapegoats, is a different thing entirely. Therefore, empathy is both a remedy for feelings of shame and an ally to those who practice accountability. We don't have to make decisions based on the worth or value of individuals; we can make decisions based on the objects themselves.

Shame might keep us from seeing who we are in Christ, while being praised can help us remember who we are.

Shame serves to conceal who we really are. It's not because things have a nice appearance that Peter encourages us not to be ashamed of them. Because we are called by His name, Peter directs our worship toward Jesus. As Christians, it should not come as a surprise that we endure hardship. What is astonishing is that we would let the challenges we confront, whether they come from the outside world or from our own people, bring down the value we hold for ourselves. And when we are in a position of leadership, we are aware that even when we are engaging in inappropriate behavior,

Inquisitiveness and firm assurance

Leaders who are effective exhibit both the willingness and the bravery to navigate "the gray." This needs us to be able to navigate the ambiguity of paradoxes and opposites that we are confronted with in practically every leadership decision, such as having a huge heart while making severe judgments, thinking big while starting small, being optimistic while remaining realistic. It is easier and less hazardous for leaders to make decisions and think in terms of "all or nothing" when they lack the confidence or bravery to lead in the gray areas. Because of this protective armor, the leader is able to remain hidden and avoid engaging in the difficult work that generates the best outcomes.

In any event, what are the benefits of engaging in this activity?

The messy process of learning and unlearning, practicing and failing, and surviving misses," as Brene Brown describes it, is the path to developing grounded confidence. This kind of self-assurance is not an act of posturing that is based on bologna. Confidence that is rooted in reality is genuine and is developed by self-awareness and EXERCISE. Leaders need the grounded confidence to

(1) Stay true to their values,

(2) Respond rather than react emotionally, and

(3) Operate from self-awareness rather than self-protection when navigating the discomfort of "gray."

Tough conversations, difficult meetings, and emotionally charged decision making all require leaders to have this grounded confidence.

What is your secret to success?

Develop your "rumble" skills with self-assurance. We hate to be the ones to break it to you, but simple learning doesn't lead to robust abilities. Before even attempting a performance, the athlete or musician puts in countless hours of practice working on the fundamentals. To gain the self-assurance necessary to effectively manage gray areas, we need to engage in learning that is challenging and unsettling enough to temporarily irritate our brains. We need to put ourselves in challenging situations so that we can "feel the burn" and build up enough "muscle memory" in our brains to be able to handle challenging circumstances on auto-pilot.

Remain curious. Our minds are set free from predetermined results or confines when we have a strong desire to know more and gain new information. It is possible for leaders not to have the intestinal fortitude to have difficult conversations since they are unable to control either the path or the conclusion. When entering a challenging conversation, reframing the situation with an attitude of curiosity offers the leader the courage to ask questions to learn more. Rumble starters such as "I'm curious about," "Help me understand," "I'm wondering about," and "Tell me why this doesn't work for you" are helpful curiosity primers that may be utilized to create confidence in engaging others in a challenging conversation.

Practice. Practice. Practice. Only through consistent practice, particularly under trying circumstances, is it possible to gain and maintain confidence. Participate in opportunities that will force you to put yourself out there, such as leadership rounds. Be open to the feedback of your coworkers and make it a habit to practice sharing a mistake or challenging scenario you've managed. Roll play a challenging conversation with a classmate and talk about the different ways you could handle the flow of the interaction thereafter. Act. Do it again and again. The process of building grounded confidence requires a lot of practice and making mistakes.

Keeping our values in mind

To me, a leader is someone who accepts responsibility for discovering the potential in people and processes and who possesses the bravery to develop that potential in others.

This definition acknowledges that every member of an organization possesses the potential to exercise leadership, as well as the fact that leadership can involve the creation and maintenance of not only people but also tools, technologies, procedures, source code, documentation, relationships, and cultures.

A belief system or way of being that is significant to us is referred to as a value.Leaders should always exhibit a clarity of values, and that leaders should do more than just preach their values; rather, they should act in accordance with their ideals. As leaders, we have an obligation to be transparent about what it is that we value and think to be essential, as well as to ensure that our actions, thoughts, and words are congruent with the beliefs and values that we hold. Reflection and thought are very personal activities that many people have never taken the time for, but they are necessary steps in the process of explicitly identifying our beliefs. I thought it would be beneficial for me to define and express my core values, and I thought it would be beneficial for each member of my team to do the same, as a way to improve self-awareness, understand each other better, recognize opportunities for leadership, and support each other in our values. This activity is one in which we investigate, identify, express, and discuss the values that are most important to us; this essay is an investigation of that exercise.

The list consists of more than one hundred distinct ideals and principles, such as accountability, achievement, balance, competence, excellence, family, giving back, joy, legacy, order, patience, recognition, resourcefulness, travel, wealth, and wisdom. In addition to that, you can provide your own values. The goal of this exercise is to distill this extensive list of values down to your top two guiding principles.

Narrowing this list down to just two core principles is an extremely challenging task. The majority of people can identify with ten to twenty core values. If, on the other hand, several of the values on the list are significant to you, then nothing on the list can be considered a driver. The process of narrowing the list of values that you identify with, which we refer to as values of the second tier, down to just two is one of the most challenging tasks.

After going through this exercise myself and observing a number of my friends and coworkers go through it, I believe that the most effective way to focus our values is to first identify all of the values that we connect with and then organize them into values that relate to each other. This was my conclusion after going through this exercise myself and watching a number of my friends and coworkers go through it. With the use of this mapping, we were able to identify our driving values, which are supported by our other values.

When people are willing to stay with the process long enough to whittle down their big list to two, they always come to the same conclusion that I did with my own values process.

Exploring My Values

The following is an underlined list of the values that I identified with. In addition to that, I added three of my own: objectivity, diligence, and high quality. Time is yet another value that, in the absence of further clarification, is susceptible to being misunderstood. I place a high value on having time to work independently or with a select few others in an intimate setting, where I can concentrate, get into the zone, and produce in-depth, difficult, high-quality work. The act of switching between different contexts or making impulsive decisions without taking the time to digest, contemplate, or experiment is not something that I particularly enjoy doing. It is not fun for me to make investments with a short-term horizon without first considering the effects those investments will have on the larger system or how they will fit in with my long-term goals. In my position as a manager, which requires me to cope with a broken schedule and make myself available for interruptions, I frequently find that this aspect of my job is in contradiction with other responsibilities. It is also in conflict with the distracting open-plan offices that are so prevalent in today's society, as well as the never-ending stream of email, group chat, code reviews, and other forms of digital communication. The fact that I am responsible for operating essential, customer-facing production services and that I may have to respond to a production incident at any moment also affects how highly I value my time. There are times when the mere expectation of being interrupted is sufficient to ensure that I will have difficulty getting my work done. Take note of the way in which connecting values with other values helps to give them more texture and makes it easier for other people to interpret them. A few core beliefs that resonated with me on multiple levels. For instance, time in terms of the quality of my time and the experiences I have, as well as time in terms of the opportunity to learn and increase my level of expertise. I identified not only with understanding and knowledge, but also with vulnerability in terms of how poorly I felt I was understood by other people.

As I dug deeper into these four core values—quality, independence, knowledge, and vulnerability—it became abundantly clear to me that the value I placed the most importance on was quality. It served as the impetus for virtually all of my other core values. As I delved deeper into the topic of vulnerability, I came to the realization that the values I associated with it were also concerned with quality. These values included the quality of my relationships, the quality of the experiences that I have in common with other people, and the quality of the organizations of which I am a part Choosing only two of my values to focus on was challenging. There was no question in my mind that quality was the most important value, but I also placed a high premium on independence and knowledge. Knowledge was the option that was recommended to me by one of my coworkers, who pointed out that independence cannot exist in the absence of knowledge. On the other hand, I come to identify with these principles from the opposite direction: it is because I have knowledge that I am able to be free, express my creativity, take chances, and be original. Knowledge is the second core value that I've identified with the assistance of my coworker.

Putting Forward My Two Fundamental Principles

Organizing your second-tier values around your two core values, as I've mentioned before, helps give them texture and makes it easier for other people to understand them:

When you have determined your two most important values, you should then formulate a sentence for each one that can succinctly convey this value to another individual. Quality and knowledge are at the very center of my worldview. I place a high value not only on the quality of my work but also on the quality of my experiences and the quality of the connections I have with others. I place a high value on knowledge because it serves as the cornerstone of comprehension and provides fuel for my aspiration, creativity, autonomy, and intuition.

Gaining strength

The same disruptive conduct permeates business culture despite the fact that businesses have invested enormous amounts of time and money into the development of their employees over the course of the past decade. It doesn't matter if it's because of the proliferation of the digital world, the growth of virtual and remote teams, or the public naming and shaming that occurs across social-media platforms; people are increasingly choosing to abandon ship rather than work through the difficulties that they face.

People frequently keep their mouths shut at work out of fear of retaliation or rejection, and according to Vital Smarts, every conversation failure costs an organization an average of $7,000. This is despite the fact that failing to speak up in a conversation costs an organization an average of $7,000. It's true that many leaders don't bat an eye when they're put in charge of budgets in the multimillion-dollar range, but just the prospect of having to deal with an employee's negative emotional reaction might be enough to make them want to avoid having that conversation. After all, feelings can get messy.

However, failing to have these dialogues results in a leadership void, which in turn has an effect on morale, employee retention, and financial results. If you choose to avoid having daring dialogues, ripples will be formed that will hamper your growth. In other words, bringing individuals on board for unpleasant conversations may generate turbulence, but because these conversations are also unavoidable, here are seven strategies to land safely with all of the passengers still in one pieceAdditionally, The Power of Uncomfortable Conversations can be found here.

Bypass one's ego.

People frequently wait until an interpersonal situation has escalated to the point that it requires Navy Seal-worthy extraction before confronting it; nevertheless, the more you postpone conflict, the more emotionally charged it will become. The strategy of waiting until there is no turning back is less proactive than interrupting a habit of conduct as soon as it is seen. You'll want to make it a practice to have dialogues that are open, honest, and transparent as soon as possible once an issue has come up. The more you talk, the more comfortable it will be for you to have talks in the future.

The King Is in the Preparation

It is absolutely necessary to devote some time to formulating a strategy for dealing with potentially difficult circumstances that do not go according to plan. Conversation that is completely rehearsed can give the impression of insincerity and lack of authenticity. Instead, devote your effort to formulating insightful questions that can assist you in comprehending how the scenario developed and the parts that each individual played in it. Make an investment in preventative measures and the opportunities they present.

Take a Step Back from Behavior

It is more beneficial to try to understand someone's intent rather than trying to take over the conversation with blame and shame. In a recent essay published in the Harvard Business Review, the author emphasized the need of setting the appropriate energy before to engaging in a challenging conversation by asking oneself, "What's the best method for this person to hear the message?" It is possible to create an opening for introspection by starting a conversation with someone about how their life is currently going for them. Anger and introspection are mutually exclusive states of mind to occupy at the same moment.

Embrace Opportunities to Teach and Learn

A significant number of leaders put off having uncomfortable talks by disregarding behavior that is inconsistent with the values of the business. This, in turn, results in the gradual accumulation of frustration over time. Emailing issues back and forth is a rather impersonal method that leaves a lot of room for misunderstanding. Engage in proactive behavior and plan face-to-face interactions.

Be Compassionate

Take the time to put yourself in the position of another person and consider the possibility that there are more aspects that have led to the current predicament. Your capacity for empathy decreases the possibility that you may respond defensively. Additionally, pay attention to whether the talk should take place at a specific time or in a particular place. The use of neutral locations can assist reduce the likelihood of interruptions or eavesdropping. Take care to pick your words, and also pay attention to the tone of your voice and the way you carry yourself. If you feel like you've been provoked emotionally, hit the stop button and take a break. It's important to be aware of your own triggers as well as the limits of your position and duty.

Put your feelings in the driver's seat.

Check in with your feelings before, during, and after the talk to ensure that you are responding rather than reacting to the other person's statements. The pace of the talk can be slowed down as an additional strategy for preventing the escalation of tensions. Your ability to organize your thoughts and select words that are congruent with your actions is much improved when you moderate your tempo.

Create Solutions Together

When there is input from both parties, there is a greater possibility that the behavior may change. After any meeting of this kind, reaching a consensus on the outcomes is an absolutely necessary step. Written confirmation quickly afterward helps eliminate uncertainty and prevent misunderstanding, and it illustrates how a tough conversation may become a positive engagement that is good for all parties involved if the participants are willing to listen respectfully and talk honestly.

www.ingramcontent.com/pod-product-compliance
Lightning Source LLC
Chambersburg PA
CBHW050328220526
45465CB00005B/2187